NORWICH

A JOURNEY THROUGH

Norwich Heritage Economic and Regeneration Trust (HEART)

Norwich 12
A journey through the English city

Published by Norwich Heritage Economic
and Regeneration Trust (HEART)
PO Box 3130
Norwich NR2 1XR
www.heritagecity.org

Norwich HEART is a private, charitable company
set up to act as an umbrella organisation for
all the city's heritage. We strategically plan,
regenerate, manage and promote Norwich's
heritage and act as a best practice exemplar
nationally and internationally for developing
heritage as a vehicle for social and economic
regeneration.

© Norwich HEART 2008

ISBN 978-0-9560385-0-0

Text by Bernadette Sheehan and Charlie Watson.
Edited, designed and brought to production by
East Publishing, Norwich.
www.eastpublishing.com

Printed in the UK by Norwich Colour Print Ltd.

Every effort has been made to seek permission
to reproduce images and text in this guidebook
where copyright does not reside with Norwich
HEART or the Norwich 12 partners. Please
contact Norwich HEART with details of
any omissions.

Front cover: exterior and interior details of
the Norwich 12 buildings (left to right, top to
bottom: Norwich Castle, Norwich Cathedral,
Great Hospital, The Halls, Dragon Hall, Guildhall,
Assembly House, St James Mill, St John's
Roman Catholic Cathedral, Surrey House,
City Hall, The Forum)
Inside front cover: Romanesque groin vaulting
in the nave aisle, Norwich Cathedral
Back cover: St Andrew's Hall
Back cover fold-out: Marble Hall, Surrey House

City plan on page 9 courtesy of Raymond
Frostick.

Producing this guidebook has been
a collaborative project in which many people
have helped with research and interviews, and
by supplying text, photography and other raw
materials. Norwich HEART wishes to thank
them all.

Photography, subject specified where more than
one photographer's work appears on a page:

Assembly House, page 63 (Assembly House)

Terry Burchall, 9 (plan)

Ricky-Joe Burrage, front cover (The Halls, St
John's Cathedral, City Hall door detail), 6 (Great
Hospital, The Halls), 7 (Assembly House,
St John's Cathedral, Surrey House, City Hall),
21 (cloister), 23, 25, 26 (windows, carvings), 27
(Blackfriars'), 38, 39, 45, 46, 47 (reredos, arch),
48, 50, 51 (Board Room), 52 (exterior), 54 (door,
lion), 55, outside back cover and fold-out

Group Archive, Aviva plc, 49

Dave Guttridge, The Photographic Unit,
Norwich City Council, 63 (The Halls)

Jarrold Publishing, 40, 42 (studio, brickwork)

Tom Mackie, 7 (The Forum), 57, 60, 63 (The
Forum)

Master and Trustees of the Great Hospital, 20

Norfolk County Council Library and Information
Service, 24

Norwich Castle Museum & Art Gallery, 8 (coins;
detail of *The South East View of Norwich Castle*,
1738, S & N Buck), 15 (painting by John Sell
Cotman)

Norwich City Council, 53

Andrew Perkins, front cover (Dragon Hall,
Assembly House, St James Mill, Surrey House,
The Forum), inside front cover, 9 (eagle), 13, 14
(Bigod Arch), 17, 18 (boss), 22, 26 (door detail),
27 (St Andrew's), 30 (lion, chamber, coat of arms),
32, 35, 37, 42 (timbers), 43 (staircase), 47 (boss),
51 (ceiling, window), 52 (cupola), 54 (chamber),
58, 63 (Norwich Castle, St James Mill)

George Plunkett, 8 (Great Hospital), 9 (Dragon
Hall), 10 (Norwich Cathedral, Guildhall), 11
(St James Mill, City Hall), 29, 33, 36, 41, 44

Chris Skipworth, front cover (Norwich Castle,
Guildhall), 6 (Norwich Castle, Norwich Cathedral,
Guildhall), 7 (St James Mill), 15 (exterior, detail),
28, 30 (flint), 43 (exterior), 63 (Surrey House)

Peter Smith, Newbery Smith Photography,
© Jarrold Publishing and Norwich Cathedral, front
cover (Norwich Cathedral), 16, 18 (choir), 19

St John's Roman Catholic Cathedral, 63
(St John's Cathedral)

George Swain, 34 (Dragon Hall c.1925)

The Forum Trust, 11 (The Forum), 56

The Photographic Unit, Norwich City Council,
6 (Dragon Hall), 34 (Dragon Hall today), 63
(Dragon Hall)

Kieron Tovell, 59

Emma Whitcombe, front cover (Great Hospital),
21 (bosses), 30 (east gable), 31, 63 (Great
Hospital, Guildhall)

Emma Whitcombe, Norwich Castle Museum
& Art Gallery, 14 (death masks, torcs)

CONTENTS

Norwich 12: a unique collaboration   6

Norwich: the last millennium   8

Norwich Castle   12

Norwich Cathedral   16

The Great Hospital   20

The Halls   24

The Guildhall   28

Dragon Hall   32

The Assembly House   36

St James Mill   40

St John's Roman Catholic Cathedral   44

Surrey House   48

City Hall   52

The Forum   56

Visitor information   60

Opening times, facilities, accessibility   61

Index   62

Map   63

NORWICH 12

A UNIQUE COLLABORATION

"All for one and one for all." Collaborations in popular literature like *The Three Musketeers* – not to mention *The Magnificent Seven* – make the point that cooperative, integrated endeavour is usually more effective than fragmented, individual action. That's certainly a view Norwich Heritage Economic & Regeneration Trust (HEART) promotes enthusiastically. HEART is a private charitable trust set up in 2004 to act as an umbrella organisation for all the fantastic and often unknown heritage in Norwich. We strategically plan, regenerate, manage and promote Norwich's heritage and act as a best practice exemplar nationally and internationally for developing heritage as a vehicle for social and economic regeneration.

We have ambitious ideas about moving the heritage agenda forward in Norwich and early on spotted a key opportunity in the city's iconic heritage buildings. The city has a host of outstanding structures and institutions, but they are often overlooked by visitors and even by local people. When we then considered how we might develop more effective heritage products in the area, our attention was drawn to Philadelphia in the United States. Here, in the Independence National Historical Park, 20 structures associated with American independence and the founding of a new nation are presented by the US National Park Service as a unified set, even though they exist under a plethora of ownership and management regimes. As a result, visitors see Philadelphia's heritage buildings as a single group, not a chaotic cocktail. And they come in substantial numbers to enjoy it – 4 million a year at the last count.

Understanding the English city

From this seed of inspiration sprang Norwich 12. Where Philadelphia has a unique opportunity to tell the story of the American Revolution through its buildings, so the iconic buildings of Norwich show the evolution of the English city over the last 1,000 years – from the time of the Normans, when perhaps we could argue that the modern English city has its roots, to the turn of the new millennium.

What makes Norwich 12 unique? Simply that it's the UK's finest collection of individually outstanding heritage buildings spanning the Norman, medieval, Georgian, Victorian and modern eras. The buildings are individually exceptional, but as a group they form a unique evocation of the English city as seen through its great institutions. Not only do the buildings have great architectural value, but they house important religious, civic, commercial and other institutions which have helped to shape the city's development, as well as cultural collections of international significance. Rather than standing in ruins, each building continues to play a pivotal and thriving role in city life, whether as a visitor attraction, a corporate headquarters, a community building or a place of worship or learning.

But we still had to move Norwich 12 from concept to reality. That transformation began in 2006, when HEART secured almost £1 million from the Treasury's Invest to Save Budget (ISB) to launch the scheme. The goal from day one has been to develop these 12 iconic buildings into an integrated family of heritage attractions which will act as an internationally important showcase of English urban and cultural development over the last 1,000 years. We're currently seeking additional funding to help sustain the project beyond the initial three-year ISB project period.

Walk, browse, climb, survey, explore!
Today the task is well under way: Norwich 12 is a dynamic, exciting collection that offers something for everyone. You can visit the 12 buildings on foot, either independently or with a guide. There are visitor attractions, exhibitions, music and performances to enjoy. You can browse in the gift shops, and eat and drink in the cafés and restaurants. There are even some extreme heritage experiences to try – you can climb the towers of City Hall and St John's Cathedral, or survey the city from the castle battlements. And if you're feeling brave, you can explore the wonderfully dark and ancient recesses beneath some of these historic structures.

Meanwhile, the work of developing Norwich 12 continues. This guidebook will help promote the message that Norwich 12 is a set of unique-but-linked institutions – not a dozen separate destinations but a single, multidimensional experience spanning 1,000 years. We're also aiming to raise the profile of individual buildings that in the past haven't registered on visitors' radar.

As well as the guidebook we've put in place a range of other initiatives, including:

- a dedicated website (www.norwich12.co.uk) – individual historical websites for all 12 buildings are in the pipeline
- a free leaflet
- an integrated events programme
- a film creating a visual journey around the 12 buildings, shown on plasma screens in the buildings themselves and online
- new interpretive signs, including innovative technology that enables free information downloads to mobile phones
- guided walks and self-guided trails
- virtual reality models of the buildings, in some cases showing how the site looked hundreds of years ago
- special tours (associated with Heritage Open Days), promotional events and exhibitions
- education projects, including an education pack on the Guildhall and a children's adventure book about Norwich Cathedral, *The 3 Serpents of the North Door*
- a communications and marketing plan which has seen the set showcased in national and international media features, travel trade journals and in local press, radio and TV
- a conservation management plan for each site to help ensure that future changes get the best out of the buildings
- support for a range of events connecting the venues, including the Go Elephants! art trail, the Norwich Ice Sculpture Trail, NORWICHRISTMAS and, in February 2009, the city's first ever Dragon Festival

Together, these elements are consolidating the Norwich 12 group and raising the city's profile as one of Europe's sensational heritage destinations. We hope they will give you a new insight into Norwich 12 and help you to discover a fantastic city and its inspiring heritage.

Michael Loveday
Chief Executive, HEART

NORWICH:
THE LAST MILLENNIUM

THE STORY OF NORWICH IS A TURBULENT AND
EXCITING ONE WHICH HAS DEFINED THE SHAPE AND
APPEARANCE OF TODAY'S CITY. THE NORWICH 12
BUILDINGS BRING THAT 1,000-YEAR STORY TO LIFE

One thousand years ago, in the early 11th century, Norwich was a thriving, fast-growing town. It contained a mint (the earliest reference to the settlement is a coin minted in 'Norvic' during the reign of Aethelstan, 924–39) and was important enough to attract the attention of King Sweyn Forkbeard of Denmark, who in 1004 "came with his fleet to Norwich and completely burned and ravaged the borough" (*Anglo-Saxon Chronicle*).

Long before this, the area had been home to neolithic (c.5000–2500 BC) and Bronze Age (c.2500–700 BC) people, and to the Romans, who established a town at Caistor St Edmund, just three miles from today's city centre, in the first century AD. Then, in the eighth century, small settlements in the Wensum valley merged to form the town that became Norwich. The Saxons who lived here, and the Danes who ruled the east of England from 869 to 917, created the busy *burh* (borough) raided by Sweyn Forkbeard.

Despite the destruction of 1004, Norwich continued to grow. By mid-century the city had between 25 and 40 churches for a population of 5,000–10,000, a busy wharf on the south side of the river near today's law courts and a principal market at Tombland (the name has nothing to do with tombs, but means open or empty space in Old English). Then came a development that had a dramatic effect on the city: the Norman Conquest of 1066.

Within a few years a new borough for the city's expanding French community had been laid out to the west of the existing settlement. Set out around a large market place, with two principal streets (today's Bethel Street and St Giles Street) leading westward, the borough shows how important Norwich was in Norman England. A significant Jewish quarter developed soon afterwards. The Normans were also quick to build a castle that confirmed their hold on the city. Work began around 1067 on defensive earthworks for a timber fortification and by 1075 the castle was able to withstand a three-month siege, after the Norman Constable, Ralph de Guader, had rebelled against the king. Work on the stone keep that survives today began around 1094. In the same year Herbert de Losinga, Bishop of East Anglia, moved the seat of the bishopric to Norwich, raising the city's profile still further. Work on a new cathedral started in 1096.

Gold-working on The Forum site	1004 Sweyn Forkbeard sacks Norwich 1067 Motte and wooden castle built 1075 Three-month siege of the castle 1096 Cathedral started	1100 Bishop's Palace started beside Norwich Cathedral 1121 Stone castle keep completed 1122 Henry I spends Christmas at the castle (below)	1145 Cathedral completed 1174 Army of Flemings occupies the castle 1175–1200 Stone houses built on The Forum and Dragon Hall sites 1194 Norwich receives charter from Richard I	1216 French Dauphin Louis captures the castle and holds it for a year 1220 First Shirehouse on castle mound	1248 College of St Mary founded on Assembly House site 1249 Great Hospital (below) founded 1250 Castle barbican ditch built 1256 Carmelite friary founded on St James Mill site
900	**1000**			**1200**	
	1000 Lief Erikson lands in North America 1066 Norman Conquest of England 1086 Domesday Book completed 1096 First Crusade		1170 Thomas à Becket murdered at Canterbury	1215 Magna Carta signed by King John 1240 The Mongols capture Moscow	

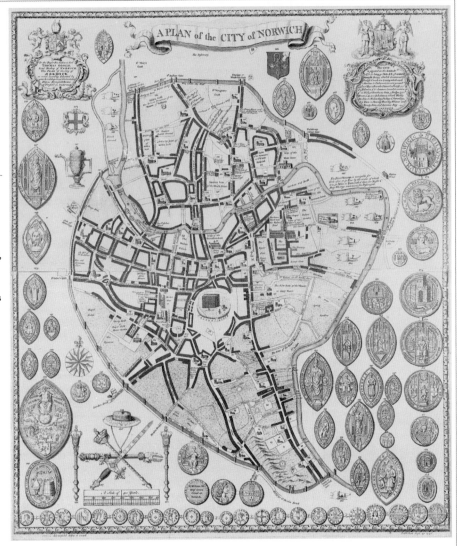

A Plan of the City of Norwich, 1746, by Francis Blomefield, including a dedication to the Bishop of Norwich, the arms of the bishopric, the deanery and the city, and numerous seals and coins

1260 Sack Friars build St Andrew's crypt and Becket's Chapel
1272 Norwich riot destroys parts of cathedral priory
1288 Church of St Mary in the Fields built on Assembly House site
1290 Tollhouse with brick vault (surviving) built on site of Guildhall

1307 Black Friars take over early St Andrew's buildings
1310 Chapter House built at St Andrew's
1325 Cathedral's Ethelbert Gate built
1325–45 Black Friars' church and friary under construction

1300

1330 John Page builds (surviving) brick undercroft on site of Dragon Hall (below)
1362 Replacement cathedral spire collapses for first time

1382 Carmelite friary church consecrated adjacent to St James Mill site
1383 Eagle Roof (detail below) at Great Hospital dedicated to Anne of Bohemia

1424 Guildhall completed
1430 Dragon Hall built
1430 Cathedral cloisters rebuilt
1440–70 Major reconstruction of St Andrew's
1450 Great Hospital cloister, Master's Lodge and St Helen's nave and tower built

1400

1460 Church of St Mary in the Fields rebuilt – the largest in the city
1462 Blackfriars' tower built
1472 Bishop Lyhart completes vaulted cathedral roof
1487 Henry VII holds court at cathedral priory

1271 Marco Polo begins tour of China
1284 Legend of the Pied Piper of Hamelin begins

1309 Construction of Alhambra in Granada
1325 Aztecs found Tenochtitlan (Mexico City)

1347 Black Death begins in Europe
1363 Tamerlane begins conquest of Asia
1387 Chaucer begins to write *Canterbury Tales*

1415 English defeat French at Agincourt
1431 Joan of Arc burned by English in Rouen

1454 Gutenberg produces first printed bible
1492 Columbus lands in the Americas

9

Over the next century Norwich continued to grow in size and importance. In 1194 Richard I (the Lionheart) granted the city a charter that gave citizens the right to select their own reeve, or ruler. A great medieval city was emerging. By the time of the Black Death in 1349, writes Brian Ayers (former County Archaeologist for Norfolk), "an urban area some 1.5 miles from north to south and 1 mile from east to west, bounded by a defensive wall and ditch on three sides, stands on both banks of the river Wensum, which is itself crossed by no fewer than five bridges. Within the defended area is a royal castle, a Benedictine monastery and cathedral, four large friary precincts, several hospitals, nearly sixty parish churches, a commercial waterfront, warehouses, markets, houses of an affluent merchant class and homes of the urban poor. The city is larger in area than London and Southwark combined and, although its population is inferior to that of London, at about 30,000 is still exceptional for the Middle Ages."

Among the great surviving buildings of this era are four members of the Norwich 12 group: the Great Hospital; the Halls complex (St Andrew's Hall, a Dominican friary from 1307, and Blackfriars' Hall); the Guildhall, the centre of city government for more than 500 years; and Dragon Hall, a spectacular trading hall built in the early 1400s by Robert Toppes, a wealthy merchant and four times mayor of Norwich.

The cosmopolitan nature of the city was boosted in the 1560s and 1570s by an influx of Dutch, Flemish and Walloon immigrants, many of them weavers. In 1570, their presence provoked an unsuccessful rebellion, led by John Throgmorton. By 1579 the 'strangers' accounted for a third of the population. Although Norwich was and continued to be an important agricultural centre, the textile industry was an essential element in its status as England's second city. Historian Frank Meeres reports that in the 1620s one in three new freemen was connected to the textile trade, rising to about half in the 1670s. In 1698 Celia Fiennes, the traveller and author, wrote that "the whole city looks like what it is, a rich thriveing industrious place".

The wealth and status of the city is shown in the number of fine buildings in the city that date back to this period and the Georgian era that followed. Among these is the beautiful Assembly House, built in

1520 Cardinal Wolsey and Catherine of Aragon visit cathedral 1531 Protestant martyr Thomas Bilney held in the Guildhall before his execution	1539 Benedictine priory at cathedral (below) dissolved 1540 Earl of Surrey's Palace built on site of Surrey House 1549 Robert Kett's rebel army occupies the castle 1578 Elizabeth I visits Norwich, staying at the Bishop's Palace	1617 Castle Fee becomes Cattlemarket 1643 Castle defences reinforced 1653 Cromwell visits the Guildhall (right) and castle 1671 Charles II visits the cathedral		1712 Blackfriars' tower collapses 1755 Thomas Ivory converts the 'Chapel in the Field House' to create the Assembly House	1792 New prison by Sir John Soane built beside castle keep 1792 James Smith produces the first recorded 'stock shoes' on the site of City Hall

1500   **1600**   **1700**

1503 Leonardo da Vinci paints Mona Lisa 1514 Portuguese begin trading in China 1534 England breaks with Catholic Church; Reformation begins		1619 First black slaves are employed in colony of Virginia 1642 English Civil War begins	1588 Spanish Armada defeated 1666 Great Fire of London 1682 French establish Louisiana colony in North America	1709 Abraham Darby's technique of smelting iron with coke starts the Industrial Revolution	1769 James Watt invents the steam engine 1789 George Washington elected 1793 Louis XVI guillotined in France

1754–55 as a centre for concerts, balls and other assemblies for the gentry of Norwich. With the coming of the Industrial Revolution (in the late 18th and early 19th centuries), England's northern cities became the engine for the country's economic growth. Their fast-flowing water and coal resources gave these cities a strong competitive advantage and the textile trade in Norwich suffered accordingly. But out of this misfortune came another great building: St James Mill. The mill – "the noblest building of the English Industrial Revolution", according to architecture critic Ian Nairn – was built by the Norwich Yarn Company in 1836 to give the city's textile industry a fighting chance.

But soon another business was establishing itself as a dominant force: insurance. The Norwich Union had been founded in 1797, had grown to national prominence and, in the late 1800s, was planning Surrey House, a handsome new building in Surrey Street. Work began in 1900 and the company's new headquarters opened for business in 1912.

On the other side of the city, meanwhile, a striking new Roman Catholic church, St John's, was being built. The new church,

later a cathedral, was a gift from the Duke of Norfolk and yet another sign of the confidence and prosperity of Norwich in the late Victorian and Edwardian eras. The city's secular fathers were soon planning a new headquarters of their own, City Hall, which was first decided upon in 1919 and finally opened by King George VI in 1938. The imposing exterior and art deco interior are today at the heart of civic life in Norwich.

In the post-war years, the city has undergone enormous change and renewal. While some traditional industries remain, the economy has diversified enormously, with creative and high-tech industries establishing themselves and the University of East Anglia, founded in the 1960s, bringing a new dynamism. In the Norwich 12 group the symbol of this change is The Forum, an award-winning, 21st-century home to BBC East and the Norfolk & Norwich Millennium Library.

Over the last 10 centuries Norwich has experienced war and rebellion, poverty and prosperity, stability and change. Without being exactly the same, its evolution echoes and complements the stories of cities across the country. Norwich 12 is truly a journey through the English city.

1824 First Norfolk & Norwich Festival held in St Andrew's Hall 1836 St James Mill (below right) started 1840 Franz Liszt performs at the Assembly House 1847 Jenny Lind performs at St Andrew's Hall	1874 Becket's Chapel at St Andrew's demolished 1876 Assembly House becomes a high school 1884 Foundation laid for St John's Roman Catholic church	1908 Sir Edward Elgar conducts the *Dream of Gerontius* at St Andrew's Hall 1909 Edward VII confers the title of Lord Mayor for the first time, in St Andrew's Hall 1910 St John's Roman Catholic church completed	1912 Surrey House completed 1938 City Hall (below right) opened by George VI 1939 Assembly House becomes Army Camouflage School 1950 Assembly House restored 1963 Queen Mother opens award-winning library on the site of The Forum	1976 St John's Church consecrated as a Catholic cathedral 1994 Fire destroys city library on The Forum site 1995 Assembly House fire	2002 Queen opens The Forum (below) and the newly refurbished castle 2006 Dragon Hall restoration complete

1800 | **1900** | | | | **2000**

1819 Simon Bolivar begins series of campaigns to free South America from the Spanish	1825 First passenger railway established 1886 First petrol engined automobile patented by Karl Benz	1908 First powered flight	1914 WWI begins 1917 Russian Revolution 1939 WWII begins 1963 President Kennedy assassinated	1990 Berlin Wall falls 1994 Channel Tunnel opens	2004 The European Union admits 10 new member countries

NORWICH CASTLE 1067–1121

NORWICH CASTLE IS ONE OF THE FINEST SURVIVING
SECULAR NORMAN BUILDINGS IN EUROPE. BEGUN
BY WILLIAM THE CONQUERER AND DEVELOPED AS A
PALACE BY HIS SONS, IT SERVED AS A PRISON FOR 500
YEARS AND TODAY IS NORFOLK'S PRINCIPAL MUSEUM

At the time of the Norman Conquest, Norfolk and Suffolk were the most densely populated counties in England. Norwich Castle was built by the Normans as a show of strength. In about 1067, they started building what became the largest castle mound (motte) in the country, surrounding it with deep, defensive, dry ditches.

Work on the stone keep began in around 1094 and was completed by 1121. White limestone was shipped in from Caen in Normandy and brought up the River Yare on barges. It was hoisted up onto the castle mound using a system of treadmills and pulleys. The lower floor, faced in dark flint, acted as a pedestal, raising the royal palace high above the city.

Norwich Castle keep was equally impressive on the inside. The upper floor was divided into two and the Great Hall was where the day-to-day business, feasts and entertaining took place. On the south side the royal quarters contained a large parlour, bedrooms and a private chapel. Despite its grandeur, though, no Norman kings ever lived in the castle.

Although much of the keep has altered, modern visitors can still get an insight into daily life in the castle in Norman times from surviving details such as fireplaces and garderobes (toilets). They also enter the keep today through the original entrance – the impressive Bigod Arch, which is heavily embellished with intricate carvings and sculptural figures.

Today only the mound and keep survive, but the original earthworks once covered 23 acres and included stone gatehouses, workshops, industrial areas, stables and grazing meadows. The castle's pattern of defensive ditches and baileys (open areas between the ditches) can still be seen at Castle Meadow and Cattle Market Street. As the city grew, the south bailey became the cattle market, where drovers brought in livestock from around the region.

From about 1300 Norwich Castle's military importance waned and for the next 500 years the keep was used as a prison for debtors, petty felons, prisoners of war and political prisoners, horse thieves, highwaymen and murderers. The latter three types of prisoner would only have stayed briefly before being publicly hanged, just beyond the castle bridge. Hubbard Lingley was the last person to be hanged for murder in Norwich, in 1867.

By the middle of the 18th century the prison was unsanitary and overcrowded. John Howard, the prison reformer, recorded the appalling conditions at the castle in 1777. A new prison block was built in and around the keep in 1792–93, designed by Sir John Soane, architect to the Bank of England. But it proved too small and its approach to prison management quickly became old-fashioned. A new jail was built, where each prisoner had their own cell, in blocks radiating from a jailer's house in the centre. It allowed prison officers to keep watch over the whole complex of cells and exercise yards.

Above: Victorian criminals' 'death masks' in the dungeon

Below: Iron Age gold and silver neck torcs in the Boudica Gallery

Below right: the Bigod Arch

Previous page: the interior of the castle keep today

In 1883 the county jail moved to Mousehold Heath in Norwich. A local architect, Edward Boardman, was commissioned to convert the castle keep and prison into a museum, and this opened in 1894. Many of the Castle Museum's early collections reflected the interests of its first benefactors. Its 19th-century bird collection is still valued by natural history specialists.

Today, as a museum and art gallery, Norwich Castle holds the largest and most specialised collection of paintings by the unique Norwich School of Artists, particularly John Sell Cotman. As well as impressive collections of archaeology and natural history, it also holds the world's largest collection of ceramic teapots and the largest collection of provincial civic regalia in the UK.

Top: Norwich Castle atop the Castle Mound

Above: a detail of Norwich Castle's striking facade

Right: *Mousehold Heath*, c. 1810 John Sell Cotman, watercolour. From the permanent collection at Norwich Castle

NORWICH CATHEDRAL
1096–1145

ONE OF THE MOST COMPLETE MAJOR ROMANESQUE BUILDINGS IN EUROPE, NORWICH CATHEDRAL HAS ATTRACTED VISITORS AND PILGRIMS FOR MORE THAN 900 YEARS

Bishop Herbert de Losinga laid the foundation stone for Norwich Cathedral in 1096, endorsing the fast-growing city's status and prospects. The Norman conquerors knew that grand castles and cathedrals would be powerful symbols to the English of their new masters – and would play an important part in controlling their lives.

Since Norfolk had no suitable building stone apart from flint, Bishop de Losinga arranged for Caen stone to be imported from Normandy. A canal was specially dug from the present Pull's Ferry on the river Wensum to Lower Close, to bring the stone as near to the building site as possible. When it was completed in 1145, the cathedral was the largest building in East Anglia, measuring 141 metres (461 feet) long and 54 metres (177 feet)

wide, including the transepts. It was consecrated in 1101 and served as a Benedictine priory until the dissolution of the monasteries in 1538.

Originally the interiors would have been brightly painted with images of saints, foliage and patterns, and lit by torches and candles. Today the original Norman ground plan is virtually intact, despite devastating gales, fires, riots and wars over the centuries. In 1272, for example, there was a serious riot outside the cathedral priory between the monks and the citizens of Norwich over disputed rights and boundaries. The cathedral cloisters were damaged, fires ravaged the building, and vestments, gold and silver were plundered. The dispute was so serious that King Henry III came to Norwich to resolve it.

Then in 1462 lightning struck the wooden spire, causing a fire which destroyed the cathedral's wooden roof. By 1501 this had been replaced with a Gothic fan vaulted roof, which complements the earlier Romanesque architecture, and the 96-metre-high stone spire (the second tallest in England) that visitors see today.

During the English Civil War in 1643 a Puritan mob entered the cathedral and removed everything they deemed superstitious or idolatrous, including images of people on statues, stained glass and carvings. Tombs and monuments were defaced or demolished.

A ball from a musket, probably fired by a parliamentary soldier, remains in Bishop Goldwell's tomb today. The cathedral was restored in 1660 and again in 1830.

Although each period of history has left its mark, Norwich Cathedral remains an iconic Norman cathedral, with powerful Romanesque pillars, arcading, and the largest and most beautifully decorated Norman tower in England. The earliest choir stalls date back to 1420 and feature rich carvings of flowers, foliage and tiny human faces. The folding seats have built-in ledges or misericords (from misericordia, Latin for mercy) on which the monks used to lean during long services. Unusually, the wooden cathedra or bishop's throne in the presbytery remains in its original position, facing the congregation and positioned behind the high altar, rather than to one side of it.

The Cathedral Close is the largest to survive in England and is reached from Tombland via the Ethelbert Gate, built c.1316, to the south of the Erpingham Gate, built c.1420–1435. The cathedral also has the largest surviving monastic cloisters in England, built between 1297 and 1430 to replace the Norman cloisters destroyed during the 1272 riot.

The work of today's cathedral community remains grounded in the principles of its Benedictine founders – worship, hospitality and learning. As well as holding traditional services, the cathedral is the venue for lectures, concerts and exhibitions.

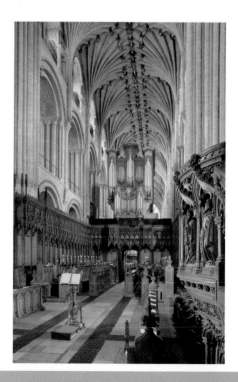

A place of inspiration

Not all cathedrals were monastic, but this one was. In fact, it was one of the biggest in Europe. The cathedral was home to a community of up to 260 monks and lay servants, whose daily life was underpinned by the Benedictine 'rule', which can be summarised in three words: worship, hospitality, learning. What happens in the cathedral today is entirely consistent with that approach to life.

But life for the early cathedral community was very different from life here today. They were sheep farmers for one thing, so their economic activity made a significant contribution to the prosperity of the city. Our contribution today is not an economic one, but one that's very valuable none the less. There have been many disturbances over the centuries – from riots and the Black Death to calamitous lightning strikes, the dissolution of the monasteries and, much later, wartime air raids – but Norwich Cathedral has come through them all. It's a truly inspiring place.

Graham Smith, Dean of Norwich

Top left: The
Erpingham Gate

Top right: Norwich
Cathedral cloister

Bottom right: The
Norman tower and
medieval spire,
seen from the
Lower Close green

THE GREAT HOSPITAL 1249

SINCE IT WAS FOUNDED IN 1249, THE GREAT HOSPITAL IN BISHOPGATE HAS HAD A CONTINUOUS, ALMOST UNPARALLELED RECORD OF CARE. THE BEAUTIFUL COMPLEX OF BUILDINGS REFLECTS THE CHANGING ROLE OF HOSPITALS OVER THE LAST 750 YEARS

When the original St Giles's hospital was founded by Bishop Walter Suffield in the 13th century, it was typical of the period. Like monasteries or priories, medieval hospitals were religious institutions and had similar layouts. They did not provide medical treatment as we understand it today, but offered their residents rest in warm and relatively clean surroundings with a regular supply of food and drink.

Many local people supported Bishop Suffield's new hospital, giving land as well as gifts and money. Benefactors believed that by endowing a hospital they would not only relieve the suffering of the less fortunate, but would also secure themselves eternal salvation. Beneficiaries of the hospital included "poor and decrepit chaplains of the Diocese". Bright but poor scholars from local schools were also given the chance to train as choristers and many went on to enter the priesthood. At least 30 beds were reserved for the sick poor (in the interests of propriety there were no female residents) and 13 paupers were to be fed daily. Masses were sung three times daily, including one for Bishop Suffield's soul.

St Helen's church is at the medieval heart of the hospital complex. It was rebuilt in the 14th and 15th centuries, and the refectory and cloister were added on the north side. The ceiling of the chancel (now the Eagle Ward) is decorated with more than 250 black eagles, painted in honour of Anne of Bohemia, who visited Norwich in 1383 with her husband, King Richard II.

Although it was a religious institution, St Giles's hospital avoided dissolution – the fate of many other English hospitals during the Reformation. Instead, the city acquired the hospital in 1547. It became known as 'God's House' and supported 40 residents. And for the first time the hospital offered medical as well as spiritual and physical care to residents. Among the permanent staff were a barber who let blood (opening a vein to allow blood to escape, a common therapeutic practice at the time), a surgeon and a bonesetter. The hospital's archives record payments for the cure of 'pockes' (probably syphilis), extracting teeth and treatments for sore legs.

Food and drink had long been recognised as an important part of medical treatment, and the residents' diets included bread and ale (made on the premises), salted fish, cheese, home-grown herbs and vegetables. Sick residents had special convalescent diets with wine and cinnamon. The changes in residents' care reflected a general shift in ideas about poor relief and the nature of charity. The Norwich Census of the Poor, taken in 1570 and the first of its kind in England, was another part of this charitable programme.

Opposite, top: vaulting and roof bosses in the Chantry chapel of St Helen's church

Opposite, bottom: the cloisters, built c.1450

Right: the swan pit, built in 1793 and in use until the Second World War

As its functions changed, so did the hospital's appearance of the. A new first-storey level was added in the chancel for women patients, and the infirmary became lodgings for male patients. The central part of the church was retained for worship, and beautiful bosses depicting religious scenes can still be seen in the chantry chapel. By the 1630s, almost 100 residents were cared for.

St Helen's House was added in 1751. The beautiful Georgian building, designed by Thomas Ivory, contains an oval hall leading to the Ivory Rooms, which feature fine domed ceilings decorated with cherubs and foliage. In 1793 a swan pit was built – from the Middle Ages swans had been bred for sale and for consumption on feast days. Birkbeck Hall, a fine example of Gothic revival architecture, was built in the early 20th century on the site of the old brewhouse.

Since the mid-19th century the Great Hospital has been managed by a board of trustees and it has continued to evolve to meet the needs of the people it cares for. Today it provides sheltered housing and a residential care home. Parts of the complex are also used for dinners, conferences and meetings.

Opposite: Eagle Ward, showing residents' cubicles and the communal dining table

Above: St Helen's Church

Above, right: the Music Room at St Helen's House

A gentler way of life

After 50 years employed by Swan Laundry, I came to the Great Hospital as a part-time caretaker and later full-time, when the trustees said my wife and I could bring our dog. It was still known to many older people as the 'Poor Man's Hospital', but an awful lot's changed since and people now come here from a range of backgrounds. We had a train driver who used to drive the steam locomotive from Norwich to London, and the former headmistress of St Felix's School at Southwold. One lady, years ago, had a gentleman friend who visited – you'd see his bike hidden in the bushes!

When I first came people were still living in the wards, but not for long. Today Ward One's the kitchen, Ward Two's the Mackintosh Room and Ward Three's the maintenance workshop. People still lived in Eagle Ward, too. I'd take the old company van to Kett's Hill Bakery on Monday, Wednesday and Friday to get the bread, and once a week I'd take Mrs Shaw, the Master's wife, to the cash and carry. I enjoyed the work and it's a wonderful place to live, really.

John Brock, caretaker (1979–86) and resident (1986–present)

THE HALLS 1307–1470

THE MAGNIFICENT FLINT BUILDINGS OF ST ANDREW'S AND BLACKFRIARS', KNOWN AS THE HALLS, ARE THE MOST COMPLETE MEDIEVAL FRIARY COMPLEX TO SURVIVE IN ENGLAND

The Halls were built more than 600 years ago as the home of the Dominicans (known as the Black Friars because of the colour of their habits). The site was originally settled by the Friars de Sacco in around 1250 but the Dominicans took it over in 1307, building a church and a priory for 60 friars.

The Black Friars lived simply, according to their vows of chastity and poverty, and so the construction work was largely funded from bequests by the people of Norwich. At the time Norfolk was one of the richest and most densely populated counties in England. The site was soon expanded and many of the earlier buildings were rebuilt, including a new church. When a fire gutted both the church and friary in 1413 they were rebuilt, and the friars occupied them again in 1449. The site was finally completed in about 1470.

After the dissolution of the monasteries in the 1530s, Augustine Steward (three times Mayor of Norwich) sent a proposition to Henry VIII in London, asking if the city could buy the Dominican friary buildings. By pledging to use The Halls for the good of the citizens, for fairs and feasting, Steward ensured the friary's survival. The original complex was put to use over the years as a school, granary, workhouse, building stores and even a mint, while the grand spaces of St Andrew's and Blackfriars' Halls provided an impressive setting for civic assemblies, ceremonial banquets, assizes (civil and criminal law courts for the county), guild meetings and public receptions. St Andrew's Hall has been the Norfolk & Norwich Festival's principal venue since 1824, when an organ was installed in the nave. The building was extensively restored in 1863 and the present Gothic porch was added. Today The Halls are still in constant use for conferences, antique fairs, markets, weddings, concerts and the largest provincial beer festival in the country.

The Halls' layout is typical of a medieval English friary church, including a large nave (St Andrew's), used for preaching to congregations, and a smaller chancel (Blackfriars'), where the friars held their own services. The Dominican order's religious beliefs were expressed in the simplicity of The Halls' architecture. The pillars of the nave were kept as light and as high as possible to maximise vision and acoustics, and the impressive hammer beam roof of St Andrew's Hall (a gift of Sir Thomas Erpingham, who commanded the English archers at Agincourt) is completely plain, unlike the roof at St Peter Mancroft church, built 1440–1460, which is decorated with fan vaulting and carved angels. The west window is Victorian Gothic and the stained glass features the coats of arms of well-known local families.

Opposite:
St Andrew's Hall, originally the nave of the medieval friary church

Right: a late 17th-century print of the south prospect of The Halls, showing the original central tower, priest's house and outdoor pulpit

Above: The Halls are the same size and basic structure today as they were when building work began in 1325

Above right: a detail of the south door with the arms of its donors, William Paston and Margaret Maultby, his wife

Right: in keeping with the religious beliefs of the Black Friars, The Halls contain only simple carvings

Right: interior view of St Andrew's Hall, showing the size and beauty of its proportions and a fine hammerbeam roof

Below: the paintings in Blackfriars' Hall form an important part of the civic portrait collection

As usual in friary chancels there are no aisles in Blackfriars' Hall, so the great perpendicular windows are unusually high. At the east end there is a seven-light window dating from the middle of the 14th century. After the Reformation, Norwich's Dutch community worshipped here; on the north wall there is a plaque (in English and Dutch) in memory of their pastor, Joannis Elison, and his son, who succeeded him.

The crypt, now a café, is the oldest part of The Halls. It was built around 1258, probably as the friars' dormitory, and the brick-vaulted ceiling is one of the earliest in the country. The crypt doors open on to the ruins of Becket's Chapel (a small church built by the Sack Friars in the late 13th century), which have been covered and the space is used for theatrical performances. The cloisters – originally a quadrangle where the friars would have studied and meditated – house a weekly antiques market. Further remains of the cloisters can be seen outside, on the north side of the building.

My kind of concert hall

St Andrew's and Blackfriars' Halls are the kind of building I love very much: high ceilings, lots of light and lots of wood. Old buildings are a pleasure to work in. In the 14th and 15th centuries they needed such spaces for their beautiful singing. If the ceiling was too low, they were not so close to God. But in many buildings today the ceilings are just above your head, so there's no room to do anything and it creates an oppressive sound.

I have very good memories of the workshops I've led in The Halls. They were gatherings of disparate people who came together to make music, which is a beautiful and civilised act. There have been some charming moments, too. On one occasion there was a rainstorm outside and people took shelter and inadvertently had to listen to music! They were astounded by what they discovered.

Sir Colin Davis CH, President and former Principal Conductor of the London Symphony Orchestra

THE GUILDHALL 1407–1424

NORWICH'S MAGNIFICENT GUILDHALL EMBODIES THE CIVIC PRIDE OF ITS FIRST INDEPENDENT CITIZENS, WHO BUILT IT 600 YEARS AGO

The year 1404, when Norwich received its first charter of incorporation, was a turning point in the city's history. Norwich was one of the first towns in England to receive this right to elect a mayor, collect its own taxes, hold its own courts of law, own property in common and enjoy the full status of a city. It was then England's second city, with a population of around 10,000.

To celebrate these new freedoms, a splendid new civic building was erected to house council meetings, law courts and all the other aspects of city government. The Guildhall was by far the largest and most elaborate medieval city hall ever built outside London. Closer in scale and design to the great city halls in the wealthy cloth towns of the Low Countries (with which Norfolk had close trading contacts), it was a statement of economic and political power by the emerging ruling elite – wealthy freemen who were merchants and traders.

The Guildhall was built between 1407 and 1424 on the site of a Norman tollhouse. It resembles a church in plan, with the Great Chamber (nave) and Council Chamber (chancel) built in two separate units. The exterior is an excellent example of the knapped and galletted flint work for which Norwich is famous, particularly the east end, which is chequered with alternate squares of faced flint and ashlar stone, replicating the 'exchequer' on the London Guildhall.

In the 19th century the exterior of the building was extensively altered. The Guildhall's clock tower was erected in 1850 and the stone doorway on the south-west corner was added. This originally belonged to a house on London Street owned by John Bassingham, a Tudor goldsmith. In 1861 many of the windows were replaced in the Victorian Gothic style.

From 1413 until 1938, when the new City Hall (see pages 52–55) opened, the Guildhall housed all the civic assemblies that regulated the lives of Norwich's citizens. The assembly chambers were also used as law courts until 1985, when a new court complex opened, and covered everything from minor disputes through to the most serious offences.

Inside, today a café occupies what was the original 'free prison' where unshackled prisoners were kept until 1597. Later the room became a yarn hall and played a vital role in the city's textile industry. In the mid-18th century it became the Court of Record and housed the county assizes. Much of the structural work and panelling dates from this period. In 1985 the old Georgian courtroom became the Tourist Information Centre, until this was relocated to The Forum in 2002. The Guildhall shop formerly housed a prison and the city fire engine.

Opposite: the south side of the Guildhall today

Right: the Guildhall by night in 1935, decorated for the silver jubilee of King George V

Top: impressive flint chequerwork on the east gable

Above left: oak carving in the Council Chamber, dating from 1534–7

Above right: the Council Chamber, used until 1938

Right: stained glass detail and the city's coat of arms in the Council Chamber

Far right: detail of the Guildhall's flint exterior

Right: the Sword Room, containing a virtually intact Victorian courtroom which was in use until 1985. The figure of Justice dates from the 18th century

Other parts of the Guildhall are normally not open to the public, but they too provide fascinating evidence of its history. A 14th-century undercroft, part of the old tollhouse, extends under the cycle racks at the end of the building and was used as a dungeon until the 17th century. Its most famous prisoner was Thomas Bilney, the Protestant martyr, who was burned for heresy in 1531. The brick-built undercroft, possibly one of the very earliest in England, was last used in the Second World War to protect the city's records and regalia.

The Great Chamber above the Georgian courtroom was originally used for meetings of the full medieval council (about 100 members). It now contains a virtually intact late Victorian courtroom, which was used for the city's quarter sessions. Among the cases tried was that of 8-year-old William Tuck, sentenced in 1839 to transportation to Australia for the theft of two bottles. The Great Chamber is also known as the 'Sword Room' because of its 18th-century use as the city's armoury of pikes and muskets.

The beautiful Council Chamber, originally designed for meetings of the 24 aldermen (senior councillors) of the mayor's council, was also used as the mayoral court. The room features 16th-century oak panelling below the east window, a 16-bay roof with tie-beams and ornamental decoration, and stunning stained glass windows.

In the basement under the café is the 'clink', where shackled prisoners were kept. It remained a prison, supporting the various courts, until the 19th century, when it was converted to police cells. These were in use until the late 1980s and still bear the occupants' graffiti.

The murder of Martha Sheward

In June 1851 body parts were discovered near Martineau Lane, the Aylsham Turnpike (Road) and Hangman's Lane (Heigham Road). The remains were held at the Guildhall, where surgeons examined them and declared the victim a woman of 16 to 26. While the press speculated wildly and the mayor appealed for information, the body parts were preserved in a pan of 'spirits of wine'. In 1856, with the trail gone cold, they were buried in the vaults beneath the building.

In 1869, out of the blue, a Norwich publican, William Sheward, walked into Walworth police station in south London and confessed to the murder of his wife, Martha. He was swiftly brought to the Guildhall in Norwich and charged, and the buried body parts were exhumed. Although he retracted his confession, there were no witnesses, there was no forensic science to confirm the victim's identity, and his wife's age in 1851 had been 54, the jury found him guilty. He was hanged on 20 April 1869 at Norwich City Gaol (where St John's Cathedral stands today), and buried in the grounds. The victim was reburied beneath the Guildhall.

Maurice Morson, Detective Chief Superintendent and Head of Norfolk CID (retired 1987)

DRAGON HALL c.1430

DRAGON HALL IS UNIQUE IN WESTERN EUROPE AS THE ONLY SURVIVING MEDIEVAL TRADING HALL BUILT BY AN INDIVIDUAL MERCHANT, RATHER THAN A GUILD

When Robert Toppes (c.1405–1467) built his magnificent trading hall on King Street in around 1430, Norwich was one of the largest and richest cities in the country. In 1404 it had been granted the right to elect a mayor and the city quickly embarked on a series of ambitious schemes to display its wealth, including the building of a new guildhall (see pages 28–31).

Toppes was a rich merchant who needed an impressive building to store and display his merchandise. Customs records show he regularly shipped goods from Great Yarmouth to ports in northern France, Holland and Belgium. He exported locally produced worsted cloth (used for cheap, colourful clothes), and imported luxury goods such as fine clothes, wines and spices, as well as timber, iron and roofing tiles. The Dragon Hall site, sandwiched between the river Wensum and King Street (formerly known as Conesford Street), the main north-south road through Norwich and into Norfolk, was the perfect site for his new premises. There is evidence that it was first settled in Anglo-Saxon times.

The 27-metre (88-ft) first-floor Great Hall, the centrepiece of Dragon Hall today, was a light, spacious room with three glazed oriel windows (which project from the wall but do not extend to the ground), a superb crown-post roof and seven bays. The northern four bays formed the main display room, while the southern three formed a more private space, perhaps where business deals were sealed. Toppes used expensive oak timbers throughout the Great Hall. He also placed 14 fine wooden carvings of dragons in the triangular spaces between the beams and arch braces (known as spandrels). Only one dragon survives: the carving that gives Dragon Hall its modern name. In its heyday the Great Hall would have been hung with tapestries and filled with tables laden with trade goods from all over

Europe. Below stairs, the ground floor rooms and undercroft provided secure warehouse space.

Toppes was not only a highly successful trader, he was also a member of an elite group who governed Norwich's affairs. An alderman (or senior councillor) for many years, he was elected mayor of Norwich four times and represented Norwich in parliament as a burgess (the equivalent of an MP). Toppes is depicted with his family in stained glass in the east chancel window of St Peter Mancroft church (on Millennium Plain), where he is buried.

After Toppes' death in 1467 Dragon Hall was sold. For about 100 years, it served as the townhouse of wealthy citizens and the gentry. However, as trade and industry spread along King Street these wealthy residents gradually moved out to estates in the country.

Opposite: the impressive oak crown-post roof in the first-floor Great Hall

Right: a pre-renovation view of the dragon carving in a spandrel in the Great Hall

By the turn of the 20th century, Dragon Hall had long been divided into smaller dwellings to create more living space. In the late 1930s the ground-floor rooms housed Swatman's Butchers, the rectory of St Julian's and St Peter Parmentergate, and the Old Barge Inn. The yards between Dragon Hall and the river were also filled with poor-quality housing to accommodate Norwich's growing population. The inhabitants of Old Barge Yard included small shopkeepers, cowkeepers who grazed cattle over the river and workers employed by the breweries which lined lower King Street. The yards and their buildings were demolished in 1937 by the city council as part of its slum clearance programme, apart from one cottage. This remains part of the Dragon Hall site today.

First listed as a Grade I historic building in 1954, Dragon Hall's life story was gradually pieced together by many dedicated historians, archaeologists, architects and enthusiasts. In 1979 the building, which was by then in a poor state of repair, was bought by Norwich City Council, which carried out essential building work. Since 1987 the Norfolk and Norwich Heritage Trust has continued Dragon Hall's restoration programme as a heritage site and educational resource.

An extensive redevelopment in 2005–6 saw a new north wing added to the building, containing facilities for school visits, meetings and functions. At the rear of Dragon Hall a glass gallery was built, through which the medieval timber and brick arches can be clearly seen. Interactive displays and an audio-guide tour help visitors explore the building and its fascinating history.

Above: the restored Dragon Hall today

Below: a farmer driving cattle back from market along King Street c.1925

Opposite, top: the carved dragon that gives the building its name

Opposite, bottom: the glazed gallery at the rear of Dragon Hall

An archaeological footnote

In 1997–98, ahead of the renovation of Dragon Hall, Norfolk Archaeological Unit carried out a major excavation. They discovered a host of fascinating things, but one strange find in the cellars was a single human toe bone – the only human remains. Had a medieval labourer had a bloody accident with a spade? Or was the toe some sort of charm or talisman? It was a mystery.

Then, in an art class, I met Doff Ransome. She told me about an archaeology project she'd worked on as a volunteer in the late '80s, when hundreds of human skeletons – many of them criminals, some with hands still bound – had been unearthed at a former churchyard near Magdalen Street and taken to Dragon Hall for sorting. When she confessed that she'd dropped a toe bone through a crack in the floorboards and hadn't been able to find it, the mystery was solved. Doff was delighted the toe was already in the record, albeit for the wrong excavation!

Natasha Harlow, Learning and Development Officer, Dragon Hall

THE ASSEMBLY HOUSE
1754–1755

"NORWICH CAN BE PROUD OF ITS ASSEMBLY HOUSE," WROTE THE ARCHITECTURAL HISTORIAN NIKOLAUS PEVSNER. "NO OTHER TOWN OF ITS SIZE IN ENGLAND HAS ANYTHING LIKE IT, EXCEPT, OF COURSE, A SPA TOWN LIKE BATH…"

The Assembly House that visitors see today dates from 1754, but its history stretches back more than 750 years. The Georgian building incorporates the layout of the medieval College of St Mary in the Fields, which was founded in 1248 as a hospital. The cloisters (now partly covered by the courtyard) and crypt (part of the present-day cellar) were built in 1278, and the hospital undercroft survives beneath the restaurant. What is now the Music Room contains the core of the medieval Great Hall, where much of the city's civic business was conducted before the Guildhall was built in 1407.

In 1544, as part of the dissolution of the monasteries, the college was closed by Henry VIII. The Hobart family, who lived at Blickling Hall near Aylsham, built a townhouse on the site in 1609. Known as Chapel of the Field House, it was used for public assemblies during court sessions and assizes (former courts administering civil and criminal law in each county of England and Wales).

The present-day Assembly House was designed by Thomas Ivory and opened in 1755. Ivory had been employed by a group of city aldermen to help realise the potential of the building and the site – their aim was to turn it into a centre for entertainment and assemblies for the gentry of Norwich.

Several of the former buildings were demolished or reconstructed to make way for the new two-storey structure, although the east and west wings, which have three storeys, were kept intact.

The Assembly House quickly got into full swing, hosting weekly card-playing assemblies, public assemblies during sessions week, when music would be provided, and, of course, dances. (Although even in the 18th century it appears there were traffic problems – ball guests were instructed not to obstruct the entrance with carriages, and to ask their servants to "drive off when informed by the porter that the company is not ready".) At the Guild Day ball in 1802, press reports noted that "the dresses of the ladies were elegant and highly becoming, chiefly of fine worked muslin. Feathers were very generally worn, with fancy caps and Spanish hats." In 1805 a grand ball was held to celebrate Nelson's "Glorious Victory off Cape Trafalgar" and the building was decked out with flags and banners. Some of the original banner fixings can still be seen on the balcony of the restaurant.

The entertainment programme wasn't restricted to assemblies, music and dance. In 1824 the Assembly House hosted a display of gymnastics, "feats of strength and juggling by Señor Antonio", and the following year Madame Tussaud staged a display of waxworks of "sovereigns, princes, queens and princesses, heroes and statesmen, poets and divines". It proved so popular that it ran for seven weeks.

Below: the Assembly House, before it was refurbished after the Second World War

Opposite: part of the Grand Hall, scene of a lavish ball to celebrate Nelson's victory at the Battle of Trafaglar in 1805

Above: fountain detail – a fine bronze of a boy with a waterlily bud, by James Woodford, 1954

Right: luxuriant plasterwork on a damask pink background in Ivory's Restaurant

Below: the exterior of the Assembly House today

By the 1830s Norwich's textile prosperity was in decline and the popularity of the Assembly House began to dwindle. The development of the railways meant that county society increasingly bypassed Norwich for London and sessions week lost its social importance. Although thinly attended, the subscription dances continued. In 1840 there was a concert by the Hungarian composer Franz Liszt and in 1851 the famous actress Mrs Fanny Kemble gave a reading.

Between 1857 and 1861 the Chapel Field estate was broken down and sold in lots. Frank Noverre established Norwich's leading dance academy on the site in 1858. The Noverre family, dance masters to the French court of Louis XVI and Marie Antionette, had fled to Norfolk in 1755. In the 20th century the Ballroom operated

as the Noverre Cinema, until this closed in 1993. The Assembly House became the site of Norwich High School for Girls from 1876 until the outbreak of the Second World War. In 1939, Oliver Messel, appointed by the War Office, used it as the headquarters of the Army Camouflage School. Messel, who became a famous costumer and theatrical set designer, encouraged the refurbishment of Ivory's

Right: the Music Room, partitioned to make two classrooms during its occupation by the Norwich High School for Girls

building. Restoration work began after the Second World War. It was funded by a local shoe manufacturer, HJ Sexton, whose vision was to return the building to its former glory by making it a centre for entertainment and the arts for the whole community.

To help him realise his dream Sexton turned to Stephen Rowland Pierce, one of the architects of Norwich City Hall (see pages 52–55). Rot and damp meant the building had to be completely redeveloped, and the refurbishment project cost almost £70,000. The Assembly House finally reopened in 1950 as an arts and social centre for the people of Norwich. Then in 1995 disaster struck when a fire swept through the building, destroying the roof and ceilings of the entrance hall and music room. Fortunately, much of the wooden panelling and Georgian plasterwork survived, and firefighters were able to salvage many valuable paintings and pieces of furniture. With the support of local businesses and friends the building reopened in 1997.

Today the rooms of the Assembly House are used for weddings, conferences, concerts, exhibitions and other events. A registered charity and arts trust, the Assembly House is also the home of many clubs and societies, including the Norwich Society. This group was founded in 1923 by some of the city's architects and archaeologists, to maintain Norwich's "beauty, history and character".

Risen from the ashes

On 12 April 1995 electrical equipment on the first floor started a blaze that destroyed the roofs of the restaurant, the Grand Hall and the Music Room, and caused terrible internal damage, particularly to original mouldings and carvings. One challenging aspect of the restoration was recreating that beautiful decor. We were helped, though, by one of the trustees, Mr Barratt, who'd been a firewatcher during the war. Having seen what incendiary bombs could do, he'd commissioned detailed interior photographs of the Assembly House, which he locked away in a bank vault.

Forty years later, those photos were a godsend. Once temporary roofs were in place, we got the archaeologists to put a grid in place and gave them the photos so they knew what to look for. Every piece was listed and we had 200 or so boxes of bits. At the end of the day, with the help of experts in moulding, gilding, carving, imitation marble painting and so on, we were able to restore the mouldings and carvings with total accuracy. The building reopened on Valentine's Day, 1997.

David Bissonnet,
Purcell Miller Tritton architects

ST JAMES MILL 1836–1839

IN PERHAPS AN UNEXPECTED LOCATION, FAR FROM THE TEXTILE TOWNS OF NORTHERN ENGLAND, ST JAMES MILL HAS NEVERTHELESS BEEN HAILED AS "THE NOBLEST BUILDING OF THE ENGLISH INDUSTRIAL REVOLUTION". ITS CHANGING USES OVER THE YEARS REFLECT THE CITY'S EVOLVING ECONOMY

The St James Mill site was earlier occupied by the White Friars (so called because of the colour of their robes), or Carmelites, who settled in Norwich in 1256. An original, probably 14th-century, arch survives, as does a medieval undercroft.

After the Reformation, the religious order was dissolved and the site was eventually divided up. St James Mill was built in 1836 in response to the crisis in the local textile trade. Between the 14th and 18th centuries Norwich had been England's principal textile-producing city and it exported significant quantities of cloth internationally. With the coming of the Industrial Revolution, however, the focus of economic growth shifted to the textile towns of the north of England. Competition intensified as the West Riding area of Yorkshire undercut prices using modern, mechanised systems. Lacking fast-flowing water and coal for steam, Norwich became isolated from technological innovation.

Growing unemployment and poverty among local spinners and hand-loom weavers led Samuel Bignold (1791–1875), Norwich mayor at the time, to call an urgent meeting to prevent further decline of the city's textile trade. In 1833 he set up a joint stock company, the Norwich Yarn Company, which built a four-storey steam-powered mill (now demolished) in 1835 on the river Wensum at Fishergate, at the east end of St Edmund's church. However, at the annual general meeting of the Norwich Yarn Company in June 1836 it was evident that St Edmund's Mill could not produce "more than one third of the yarn required by Norwich weavers". It was agreed that a second mill, twice as big, should be built.

The estimated cost of completing and stocking the new mill was approximately £70,000. Shares were £100 each – among the shareholders was the Jarrold family, who were later to become the mill's owners. The architect was John Brown, the county surveyor. Completed in 1839, the complex originally comprised six buildings – the mill itself, two weaving sheds, two engine houses (one for the mill and one for the weaving sheds) and a boiler house (with a 50-metre high chimney). Only the mill building and its engine house survive today.

St James Mill is six storeys high. One end is topped with a dome, capping a circular York stone staircase – an unusual feature in a mill of this type – which winds its way up around a hollow shaft. The architecture critic Ian Nairn described it as "the noblest building of the English Industrial Revolution". However, the

A view from the bridge. Opposite: St James Mill today

Right: St James Mill c.1940

building proved only a short-term solution to Norwich's economic problems at that time. Production levels did not significantly improve, and by 1900 only 2,000 people were employed in the trade in Norwich and all the traditional worsted weavers had left the city. Eventually, two years later, the site was bought by Jarrold & Sons for use by its printing department.

In 1904 St James Mill was leased to Caleys, the chocolate manufacturers. Increasingly the mill was leased to supply power, via the Norwich Steam Power Company. After the First World War the building was sold to the government and used as a training factory to help rehabilitate war veterans.

Jarrold & Sons bought back St James Mill and the surrounding site in 1933, and it later became a printing warehouse, factory and office complex. The mill was refurbished in 1991 (a free-standing staircase at the east end of the building won an architectural award for LSI architects) and today serves as Jarrold & Sons' head office, with several floors let to other organisations.

Top: design studio, Jarrold & Sons Ltd, c.1980

Above: detail of brickwork on the mill site

Right: exposed roof timbers on the top floor

Opposite, top: the south side of the mill

Opposite, bottom: the York stone staircase, less vulnerable than wood in the event of a fire

A building transformed

In the 1930s there was a gas works across the river, where the courts are today, so when we moved in the building was in a filthy state, inside and out. The windows were very loose-fitting! We stored stocks for our postcard business here and the old weaving sheds became letterpress buildings. We did a lot of war work: ID cards, soldiers' papers and technical enlargements of aircraft, among other things. And in the 1940s and '50s Jarrolds grew to be one of the UK's most technologically advanced printers – my father was a true innovator. He was a magistrate, too, and I remember he would ring down for the mill's old one-armed security man to get his bike out ready for him to cycle up to the Guildhall.

Since the mill's refurbishment in the 1990s and the recent redevelopment of the rest of the printing works site, the building's transformation is complete: from Industrial Revolution yarn mill to high-tech, 21st-century offices.

Peter Jarrold, at Jarrold & Sons 1956–1999, Chairman from 1976

ST JOHN'S ROMAN CATHOLIC CATHEDRAL 1884–1910

NORWICH'S CATHOLIC CATHEDRAL WAS A GIFT TO THE CITY BY THE 15TH DUKE OF NORFOLK, PROVIDING A NEW CENTRE OF WORSHIP FOR THE CITY'S CATHOLIC COMMUNITY IN THE 19TH CENTURY

Norwich's Catholic cathedral is the most complete example of neo-Gothic ecclesiastical architecture in the country. This exceptional church was originally conceived by Henry Fitzalan Howard (1847–1917), the 15th Duke of Norfolk. As England's most prominent Catholic, Henry Howard made it his personal mission to address the widespread, centuries-old prejudice against the faith and bring Catholicism back into English civic life.

In 1877, to celebrate his marriage to Lady Flora Hastings, Henry Howard chose to build a church in Norfolk, the origin of his title, "as a thank-offering to God". The site of the old city gaol in Norwich was chosen and the principal architect was George Gilbert Scott Junior, a convert to Catholicism.

The foundation stone was laid in 1884 and the church, dedicated to St John the Baptist, finally opened in 1910. In his address to the congregation, the Bishop of Northampton said, "This is no ordinary church…the majesty of its architecture, the vastness of its spaces, the endless charm of the mighty pillar, soaring arch and triumphant vault…recall the masterpieces of the Ages of Faith and challenge comparison with them." St John's was finally designated a cathedral in 1976 and today it is the second largest Catholic cathedral in the UK, after Westminster Cathedral.

The building is a particularly fine example of 19th-century Gothic revival architecture. The nave consists of 10 bays supported by massive columns and plinths carved by local sculptor James Ovens. The whole nave – more than 49 metres long and 18 metres high – is richly decorated with dark Frosterley marble from Durham, speckled with thousands of fossils embedded in the limestone.

At the crossing is a magnificent painted rood screen, carved by Peter Rendl of Oberammergau, one of the principal players of the town's famous passion play (traditional Lenten dramatisation of the life of Christ) in the early 20th century. A series of carved wooden tableaux – The Stations of the Cross by Ferdinand Stufflesser of Ortesi – line the north and south aisles, which also feature Grisaille glass windows painted in delicate tones of grey and green. During the 1970s the cathedral commissioned more Stufflesser works, including statues of the Risen Christ (wearing an East Anglian crown), Our Lady and the Infant Jesus, and some of the Christmas crib figures.

Right: until the early 1960s, when a new inner ring road was built in the city, the cathedral stood in its own 'piazza' at the confluence of five roads

Opposite: the cathedral today

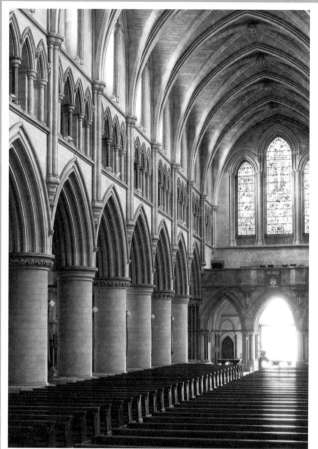

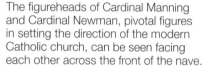

Left and below:
in early 2007
magnificent
glazed doors were
fitted inside the
great west doors.
Designed by the
cathedral architect,
Russell Taylor,
they light up the
cathedral's west
end, especially
at sunset

The figureheads of Cardinal Manning and Cardinal Newman, pivotal figures in setting the direction of the modern Catholic church, can be seen facing each other across the front of the nave.

The cathedral contains some of the finest 19th-century stained glass in Europe. Henry Howard himself designed the north transept window, known as the Queens' window. The centrepiece features Our Lady Queen of Heaven, with Esther, Judith and the Queen of Sheba from the Old Testament in the lancets. The original glass, destroyed during bombing raids in World War II, was faithfully reproduced by John Hardman & Co of Birmingham, who made most of the stained glass in the cathedral.

The magnificent window in the south transept tells the story of Pentecost and the great west window features St John the Baptist. Above the crossing is the massive tower lantern. There are regular tours of the tower, which offers a superb view of Norfolk. (During the Second World War the church was used as a turning beacon for planes returning to Norfolk after bombing assignments in Europe.)

The windows of the Sunken Chapel, or the Chapel of St Joseph, are also noteworthy. They depict Saints Flora, Pauline, Esther and Barbara – the four names of the Duke's first wife, Lady Flora Abney Hastings.

Plans to improve significantly visitor and educational facilities at the cathedral are nearing completion. A new 400-square-metre structure, the Narthex, will welcome visitors and provide for their comfort, open up the building for wider use as an arts and music venue and, crucially, allow more school visits.

Top and above right: some of the fine stone carvings in the cathedral

Above: the beautiful reredos (an ornamental screen at the rear of an altar) in the Walsingham Chapel, by Lilian Dagless

A life at St John's

I've lived near the cathedral all my life. I was baptised there 91 years ago, and made my first holy communion and was confirmed there when I was 7. I met my husband, Francis, when we were 18 and we got married at St John's on 14 April 1941. When I woke up that day my godmother said it was just an April shower, but it rained all day! My brother was a priest, and he married us.

My husband was called up for service in the war. We got married on the Easter Monday and he went back to his base the following Friday, so we only had four days' honeymoon. But that was the war, you just accepted it. When Norwich was bombed in 1942 the church windows were blown out. It was really cold during the services but we just wrapped up warm.

We had two boys and two girls, who were all baptised, had their first communions and confirmations in the cathedral, and my two daughters got married there. The church has kept me going since my husband died in 2007. I like to come every day if someone can take me.

Sybil Cushing
July 2008

SURREY HOUSE 1900–1912

MUCH MORE THAN THE HISTORIC HOME OF AVIVA (FORMERLY NORWICH UNION), SURREY HOUSE IS A SPECTACULAR PIECE OF EDWARDIAN ARCHITECTURE, RICH WITH DETAIL AND SUMPTUOUS MATERIALS

Surrey House inspires the kind of awe normally reserved for cathedrals. No other non-ecclesiastical British building can boast an interior adorned with over 15 varieties of marble, elegant stained-glass windows, classically inspired frescos, intricately carved wooden panelling, Arts and Crafts-era flourishes and a soaring glass atrium. It is a stunning blend of craftsmanship and artistry.

Construction work began in 1900 and took 12 years. Local architect George Skipper was commissioned by The Norwich Union Life Insurance Society's directors to design a "splendid yet functional office space" that incorporated Greek influences and the themes of insurance, protection and wellbeing. The aim was to reassure policyholders of the company's strength and prosperity.

The building's commanding Palladian exterior is flanked by statues of Sir Samuel Bignold (an influential descendant of Norwich Union's founder) and William Talbot (one of the founders of the Amicable Society, later part of Norwich Union).

But the most stunning feature of Surrey House is the Marble Hall. The grand entrance hall features a rainbow of shades of Greek and Italian marble, from green-grey columns to red wall panels and alabaster. Westminster Cathedral had originally ordered three consignments of this marble, but could then only afford the first, so the second consignment was instead shipped to Norwich for a knock-down £6,000. The most important pieces are the eight small pillars at the base of the innovative 'air fountain', which wafts warm or cool air around the building. These exquisite pillars are made from rare Sienna marble with a rich, rusty hue, extracted from a small quarry in Tuscany which is now worked out. The architrave around the doors on the first floor is Belgium blue marble, and an ornate 'pulpit' provides a vantage point for the hall itself and the domed ceiling.

Beyond the Marble Hall, various committee rooms display their own elegance. For example, an Adam fireplace and carved door frame (from the Earl of Surrey's original mansion on the site) grace the East Committee Room. The Board Room, meanwhile, symbolises the grand traditions of Surrey House: carved mahogany fittings, chandeliers and floor-to-ceiling windows are complemented by symbolic paintings of life, death, time and the benefits of protection.

Opposite: two teams of Italian stonemasons worked on the spectacular Marble Hall, using stone shipped in from Italy and Greece

Right: a contemporary artist anticipates the opening of Surrey House

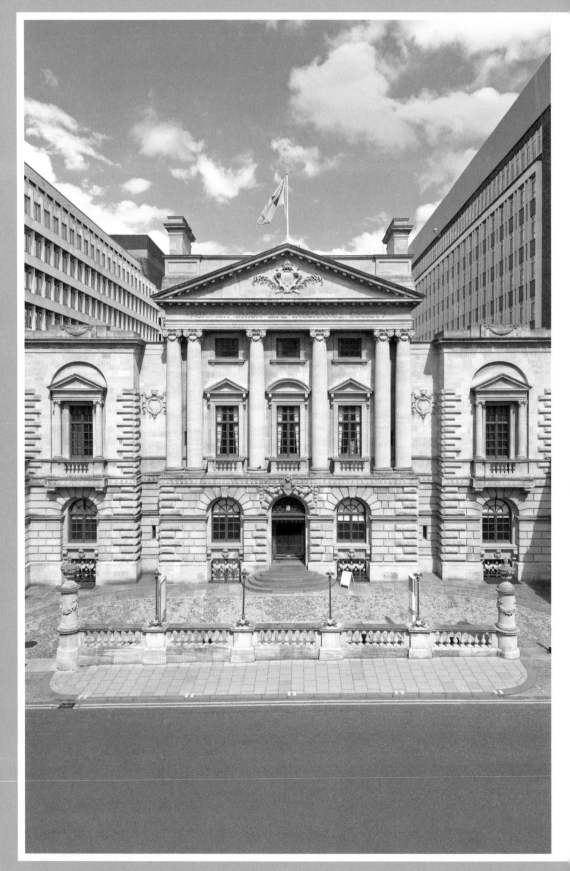

As well as its fine architectural embellishments, Surrey House contains a range of unusual items, such as a chiming skeleton clock that plays 12 operatic tunes, which was made for the Great Exhibition at Crystal Palace in 1851. In the entrance hall, striking lapis lazuli monuments honour employees who died in the First and Second World Wars, and scattered about are paintings of important figures in the company's history, including Thomas Bignold, founder of the Norwich Union.

However, while welcoming visitors, Surrey House still needs to function as an integral part of a busy modern office complex. The new atrium at the rear of Surrey House, opened in 2006, allows the building to meet the needs of 21st-century business while retaining its remarkable historic character. Featuring 200 panes of glass, the spectacular wall-to-wall skylight reveals the changing colours of the sky to staff and visitors. The 16-metre domed roof arcs above an elevated walkway, with space below for informal meetings and a café-restaurant.

The ritual of the keys

In the basement of Surrey House is a huge strongroom, where every morning, certainly until I retired in 1990, the 'ritual of the keys' took place at 11 o'clock. The two keyholders arrived at the appointed hour to allow the investment department to withdraw and deposit documents they needed. It was like Fort Knox. Those high-value documents are kept elsewhere today. Earlier, in the 1940s, the Burrows family lived in the caretaker's flat on the top floor. Mr Burrows looked after the building and his wife was a cook for the directors' dining room. Their children, Dick, Jean and Babs, had the run of the roof garden, where they'd play with their dog, Tippy, and have snowball fights in winter. Jean later trained in London as a dressmaker. When she came back to Norwich she was allowed to run her own business from the flat. People would slip in the side door and upstairs for fittings!

Don Dorling, at Norwich Union 1950–1990, retiring as Assistant Company Secretary

Opposite: Surrey House exterior

Above: the domed ceiling of the Marble Hall measures 11 metres across

Left: the mahogany-panelled Board Room is lavishly decorated with intricate carvings and paintings that symbolise themes of life, death, time and protection

Right: stained glass window and exquisitely painted ceiling on the main staircase

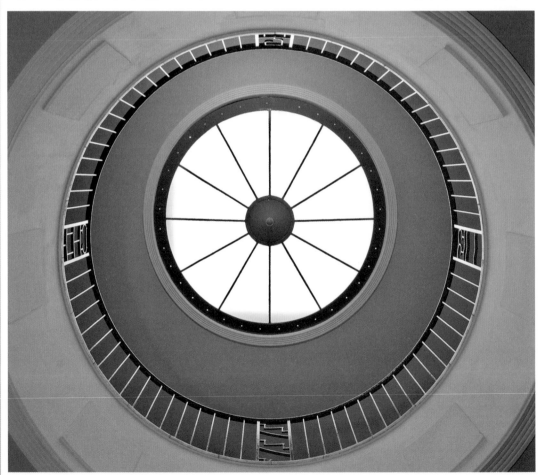

NORWICH CITY HALL 1936–1938

ARCHITECTURAL HISTORIAN NIKOLAUS PEVSNER DESCRIBED NORWICH CITY HALL AS "THE FOREMOST ENGLISH PUBLIC BUILDING OF BETWEEN THE WARS". BUT ITS BOLD DESIGN AND STUNNING ART DECO INTERIORS INITIALLY DIVIDED OPINION

When King George VI opened City Hall on 29 October 1938, it was witnessed by the largest crowd the city had ever seen. The ceremony was seen as the crowning achievement of 800 years of local self-government in Norwich. The Guildhall (see pages 28–31) had been the seat of the city's government until the early 20th century, but the council had outgrown the premises and civic business was being carried out in disused pubs and shops.

A 1908 proposal to demolish the Guildhall altogether was narrowly defeated, but wasn't until 1919 that a decision was made to build a new city hall. In 1928 Norwich City Council consulted the Royal Institute of British Architects and a national competition followed in 1931, won by London architects Charles Holloway James and Stephen Rowland Pierce. Visiting the city to talk to local architects, the prizewinners described themselves as "interlopers pinching the best job for 500 years".

Opposition to the City Hall scheme was bitter and prolonged – there were two public inquiries – but it represented only a very small minority. However, plans for the new City Hall had to be scaled back because of lack of funds – the proposed angel on top of the clock tower was dropped, and the four sides of the building were reduced to two. After claims by the council that its officials were working in rat-infested, unsuitable properties, the Ministry of Health eventually agreed to a loan of £226,000.

The foundation stone was laid in 1937 and the project became part of a larger civic-centre scheme, costing a total of £384,000. This included the redevelopment of the market and building the Garden of Remembrance. St Giles Street, Bethel Street, St Peter's Street and Gentleman's Walk were widened at the same time.

The bronze entrance doors to City Hall contain 18 plaques by James Woodward, illustrating the history, civic life and industry of Norwich. The plaques on the outer two doors display trades connected with the city – including chocolate, mustard, boots and shoes, brewing and wire-netting. There is also one to mark the building of City Hall itself. The plaques on the centre door illustrate the city's history.

Opposite top:
City Hall today, seen from the marketplace

Opposite bottom:
interior view up to the glazed cupola

Right: the winning design for the proposed new City Hall, submitted in 1932

Left: one of the three bronze entrance doors to City Hall

Below: heraldic lion designed by Alfred Hardiman

Bottom: the Council Chamber retains many of its original 1930s fixtures and fittings

Left: art deco lighting illuminates a white marble inscription listing the names of Norwich's mayors over the centuries

Flanking the entrance steps are two heraldic lions, designed by Alfred Hardiman. One of the pair was exhibited at the British Empire Exhibition of 1936, where the architects saw it and commissioned its twin. The imposing clock tower, which holds the largest clock bell in the UK, was originally intended to be visible from any part of the city. One hundred and sixty-six steps lead up to a viewing platform on the tower, which is open to the public at certain times of the year. On the exterior of the council chamber (at the rear of the building) are three figures, representing recreation, wisdom and education.

City Hall's stunning art deco interior is spread over five floors. The first-floor council chamber, a classic example of the design style, is panelled in Honduran and Cuban mahogany, while the walls of the ground-floor entrance hall (inscribed with a list of mayors since 1403) and the main landing on the first floor are lined with Italian Bianca del Mare and Nabresina marbles.

An emblem of civic pride

In 1948 I came to the City Council from Lincoln as senior solicitor and became town clerk in 1959. The building was very much as the architects had left it – the curtains in the finance department, I recall, had a pound-symbol pattern. City Hall was very fresh and impressive and at the centre of everything. Parties came from all over to visit it. The council was an all-purpose council then, responsible for education, police, water, health and so on. It was unquestionably the leading authority in East Anglia.

Weddings were also held here. At the south-east corner, the Register Office had its own door, so births, deaths and marriages were all registered at City Hall. And the civic ceremonial highlight was the annual election of the Lord Mayor, which continues today. A horse-drawn carriage brought the incumbent from his home, and the incoming Lord Mayor waited in his parlour until he'd been elected. City Hall was and is a focal point, an emblem of civic pride.

Gordon Tilsley, Town Clerk 1959–74, Chief Executive 1974–80

The top floor of City Hall has a superb glazed 'inverted cupola' that floods the building with light. The stairwell to the first floor has retained much of its original detail; the ceiling displays a fascinating painting designed by Eric Clarke and painted by James Michie, assisted by students from the Royal Academy. The image is part of a series depicting Norfolk wildlife and the city's coat of arms.

THE FORUM 1999–2001

THE FORUM IS THE LANDMARK MILLENNIUM PROJECT FOR THE EAST OF ENGLAND. A STUNNING EXAMPLE OF 21ST-CENTURY ARCHITECTURE, THE BUILDING WAS DESIGNED TO COMPLEMENT ITS HISTORIC SURROUNDINGS IN NORWICH CITY CENTRE

Forum is the Latin word for meeting place and The Forum has certainly become one of the city's central gathering places. On any dry day, Millennium Plain outside The Forum is thronged with people meeting friends, chatting or watching free entertainment in the amphitheatre. The Forum building itself plays host to a range of activities, from art exhibitions and craft fairs to commercial exhibitions and concerts, as well as being home to the busiest public library in the country.

The Forum is the landmark millennium project for the east of England and a stunning example of 21st-century architecture. Built on the site of Norwich Central Library, which was destroyed in a massive fire in 1994, the building was designed to complement its historic surroundings in Norwich city centre and serve as a cultural and recreational amenity for Norwich and Norfolk.

Sir Michael Hopkins, the architect of a number of other award-winning buildings, including the refectory at Norwich Cathedral, has created an innovative horseshoe design that embraces the immediate surroundings. The glass facade forms a stunning entrance and reflects the Gothic church tower of St Peter Mancroft

opposite, while at the back the brick casing harmonises with the smaller scale of buildings on Little Bethel Street. The handmade bricks mirror those of City Hall next door.

The Forum was officially opened by Queen Elizabeth II in 2002, as part of the Golden Jubilee celebrations and was hailed by the Royal Institute of British Architects (RIBA) as an "architectural tour de force and a major contribution to urban cultural and social life in Norwich, pulsating with the people and their activities". The building won the RIBA Award for Architecture in 2004, as well as the Civic Trust Urban Design Award (2003), and two RICS (Royal Institution of Chartered Surveyors) Awards in 2005, including eastern region Building of the Year.

Building The Forum was a £65 million project to mark the millennium. Construction was funded by a Millennium Commission grant with matching support from Norfolk County Council, Norwich City Council and the business community. The Forum's remit is to be self-funding, using a mixture of commercial partnerships and business ventures.

History, art and culture remain a fundamental part of The Forum's ethos today and the building has hosted a huge array of activities to expose people to art forms they might not seek out themselves. The Forum is also a venue for performing arts, including outdoor lunchtime events in the summer, comedy events and exhibitions within the atrium throughout the year.

Right: on the site of The Forum, archaeologists explore the city's French borough

Opposite top: a design that complements the surrounding cityscape

Opposite bottom: a stunning glass facade links the atrium with St Peter Mancroft church opposite

The atrium forms the core of the three-storey building, which houses a range of businesses and amenities arranged on a series of balconies. This covered courtyard lets light flood into the heart of the building. The impressive 15-metre-high glazed end wall opens onto the forecourt to welcome the city in, while serving as a spectacular backdrop for events and activities taking place inside.

The Forum's design helps stabilise the overall temperature, with equipment automatically monitored to ensure the most efficient use of resources. Heat from the plant room can be recycled, while the glazed atrium also acts as a return air path for the air displacement ventilation system.

The Forum is run by The Forum Trust, an independent charitable trust whose responsibilities include helping communities in the area understand, adapt to and make the most of opportunities from the growth of information technology. As a result, the way in which the building is used will evolve over time. In 2008 the south wing is being altered and improved to provide a digital media gallery and learning space, a free educational facility and resource for filming and editing and an auditorium with tiered seating for business, performance, educational and community use. To deliver these facilities, The Forum has established partnerships with the BBC and City College Norwich.

The Forum also houses the Norfolk and Norwich Millennium Library and 2nd Air Division Memorial Library, the regional headquarters for BBC radio and television, the Tourist Information Centre, a café and a restaurant.

A building for everyone

The real challenge was that the site is next to two of the city's best buildings: City Hall and St Peter Mancroft, which I think is Norwich's best church. We had to make a modern intervention. And the brief was an interesting one, calling for a public library – at a time when new libraries weren't being built – bolted on to a public meeting place, with commercial space and car parking.

But how do you respond to St Peter Mancroft? The notion we came up with was a horseshoe with the library at the back, commercial space along the sides and an 'inside-outside' space looking out at the church. The design alone won't make a building work, though. It's what happens inside. So getting the BBC interested – Greg Dyke liked the idea of a public presence – was a big step forward. The BBC, the Tourist Information Centre, Pizza Express and the many activities in the building all complement the library. The mix works very well. The life of The Forum really makes it much more than just a building.

Sir Michael Hopkins, Architect

Opposite: The Forum is home to a number of businesses and amenities, including the Norfolk and Norwich Millennium Library, the busiest public library in Britain

Above: The Forum's outdoor spaces host a range of activities all year round

VISITOR INFORMATION

THERE ARE MANY WAYS TO GET THE MOST OUT OF
NORWICH 12 AND THE CITY'S HISTORIC ENVIRONMENT.
HERE ARE FOUR STARTING POINTS

- www.norwich12.co.uk
  On the Norwich 12 website you'll
  find a wealth of images and historical
  information about the individual
  buildings, how to access and explore
  them (including self-guided walks),
  plus details of Norwich 12's education
  initiatives, latest projects, and
  an events calendar.

- Norwich 12: the film
  A new film, produced in collaboration
  with EPIC (East of England Production
  Innovation Centre) and Norwich
  University College of the Arts, creates
  a visual trail around the 12 sites. See it
  online at www.norwich12.co.uk and on
  plasma screens inside the buildings.

- Norwich Tourist Information Centre
  (TIC) in The Forum
  Tel: 0844 980 3333
  Email: tourism@norwich.gov.uk
  Norwich 12 is working with the TIC on
  a programme of guided tours of the 12
  buildings for the public and groups.
  Contact the TIC for the latest information
  on tours, advice on other places to visit
  in Norwich, and to book accommodation,
  transport and excursions. The TIC also
  stocks a wide selection of leaflets, maps,
  books, guides, postcards and gifts.

- www.visitnorwich.co.uk
  The official tourism website for the
  Norwich area. Go online for information,
  events, ideas and inspiration.

OPENING TIMES, FACILITIES, ACCESSIBILITY

Key to symbols

P Parking

Restaurant

Shop

Cloakrooms

£ Cash machine

Herb garden

Wheelchair accessible toilet

Limited wheelchair access

Disabled parking

Facilities for the partially sighted

Facilities for the hard of hearing

Café

Picnic area

Guided tours

Public telephone

Baby changing

Toilets

Wheelchair access

Ramped access

Lift

Assistance dogs

Norwich Castle
Open Mon–Fri 10am–4.30pm, Sat 10am–5pm, Sun 1–5pm. During school holidays Mon–Sat 10am–5.30pm, Sun 1–5pm. Ring to check Christmas opening times. Admission charge.
Tel: 01603 493625 (enquiries), 01603 493648
(24-hour information)
www.museums.norfolk.gov.uk

Norwich Cathedral
Open 7.30am–6pm daily (7pm mid-May to mid-September), subject to special Cathedral services. Admission free (donations appreciated).
Tel: 01603 218440, 01603 218300
www.cathedral.org.uk

The Great Hospital
This is a working building, so access to the public is limited. Tours can be arranged by appointment. The Great Hospital also runs several open days annually.
Tel: 01603 622022
www.greathospital.org.uk

The Halls – St Andrew's and Blackfriars'
The Halls are open to the public Mon–Sat 9am–5pm, subject to events (excluding Bank Holidays). The Tourist Information Centre runs tours of The Halls. All areas of The Halls can be hired for private and public events – call 01603 628477.
www.standrewshall.co.uk

The Guildhall
Parts of the ground floor are normally accessible Monday to Saturday. The Tourist Information Centre runs tours of the Guildhall, including the cells and crypt.

Dragon Hall
Open Mon–Fri 10am–5pm, Sun 11am–4pm (closed over Christmas period). Admission charge.
Tel: 01603 663922
www.dragonhall.org

The Assembly House
Open Mon–Sat 8am–9.30pm (earliest – later subject to events), Sun 10am–4pm (earliest – later subject to events). Admission free. Ivory's Restaurant & Café Bar open daily.
Tel: 01603 626402
www.assemblyhousenorwich.co.uk

St James Mill
This is a working building, so access to the public is limited. Visit www.norwich12.co.uk for information on the latest open days and tours.

St John's Roman Catholic Cathedral
Open daily 7am–8pm. Admission free (donations appreciated). Tower tours on Saturdays in summer.
Tel: 01603 624615
www.stjohncathedral.co.uk

Surrey House
This is a working building. Members of the public who visit during office hours, Monday to Friday, are usually able to look around the Marble Hall. However, visitors should telephone in advance to book a tour.
Tel: 01603 682649

City Hall
City Hall is a working building with access to the reception areas only, during office hours, Monday to Friday. The Tourist Information Centre runs tours of City Hall and its clock tower, which offers superb views across the city.

The Forum
Open daily 7am–12pm (NB: opening hours of individual services vary – please refer to the website or telephone for further details). Admission free.
Tel: 01603 727950
www.theforumnorwich.co.uk

INDEX &
SELECTED BIBLIOGRAPHY

Assembly House.............................36–39
Aviva (formerly Norwich Union)..............49
Benedictine order 18, 19
Bignold, Samuel 41, 49
Bignold, Thomas 51
Black Death......................................10, 19
Black Friars (Dominicans)......................24
Blackfriars' Hall...............................24–27
Boardman, Edward, architect 14
Carmelites (White Friars) 41
Cathedral Close....................................18
Catholic Cathedral......................7, 44–47
City Hall..............7, 29, 39, 52–55, 56, 59
Dissolution of the
  monasteries 17, 19, 20, 24, 36
Dominican order 24
Dragon Hall 32–35
Dutch community 27
East of England Production Innovation
  Centre (EPIC)......................................7
English Civil War 18
Forum, The 29, 56–59
French community..............................8, 56
Gilbert Scott Junior, George,
  architect 44
Great Hospital 7, 20–23
Guildhall 7, 28–31, 53
Halls, The 24–27
HEART (Heritage Economic &
  Regeneration Trust)............................6
Heritage Economic & Regeneration
  Trust (HEART).......................................6
Hopkins, Sir Michael, architect..............56
Howard, Henry Fitzalan, 15th Duke of
  Norfolk 44
Industrial Revolution..................11, 40, 41
ISB (Invest to Save Budget) 6
Ivory, Thomas, architect..................23, 36
Jarrold family 41, 43
Jarrold & Sons Ltd..........................42, 43
King Street 33, 34
de Losinga, Bishop Herbert 9, 17
Liszt, Franz, composer...........................38
Marble Hall...49
Messel, Oliver..38
Norfolk & Norwich Festival 24
Norfolk and Norwich Heritage Trust 34
Norfolk and Norwich Millennium
  Library 59
Norman Conquest 12, 17
Norwich 12..6, 7
Norwich Castle................................12–15
Norwich Cathedral................7, 14, 16–19
Norwich City Council 34, 53, 56, 56
Norwich School of Artists 14
Norwich Society, The.............................39
Norwich 'strangers' 10

Norwich Union...........................11, 49, 51
Norwich Yarn Company.........................40
Pevsner, Nikolaus 36, 53
Pull's Ferry..17
Reformation, the..............................20, 27
River Wensum 17, 33, 40
Roman Catholic Cathedral...........7, 44–47
Romanesque....................................17, 18
St Andrew's Hall 7, 24-27
St Giles's hospital 20
St James Mill 40–43
St John's Roman Catholic
  Cathedral 7, 44–47
St Peter Mancroft church.....24, 33, 56, 59
Second World War 31, 38, 39, 46, 47
Sexton, HJ, shoe manufacturer 38–39
Soane, Sir John, architect.....................12
Steward, Augustine 24
Suffield, Bishop Walter..........................20
Surrey House....................................48–51
Textile industry...10, 11, 29, 33, 38, 41, 56
Toppes, Robert...............................10, 32
University of East Anglia.........................11
War Office 38
White Friars (Carmelites) 40

Anonymous 2003 *Norwich Castle: history and guide*. Jarrold Publishing
Anonymous *St James' Mill*. Jarrold Histories
Ayers, Brian 1994 *Norwich*. BT Batsford Ltd/English Heritage
Brooks, John 2008 *The Great Hospital, Norwich*. Trustees of the Great Hospital
Dragon Hall www.dragonhall.org
Dunn, Ian and Sutermeister, Helen *The Norwich Guildhall*. City of Norwich in conjunction with the Norwich Survey
The Forum www.theforumnorwich.co.uk
Frostick, Raymond 2002 *The Printed Plans of Norwich 1558–1840*. Raymond Frostick
Green, Barbara and Young, Rachel MR 1981 *Norwich: the growth of a city*. Norfolk Museums Service
James, CH; Pierce, S Rowland and Rowley, HC 1945 *City of Norwich Plan*. City of Norwich Corporation
Meeres, Frank 1998 *A History of Norwich*. Phillimore & Company
Nobbs, George 1971 *Norwich: a city of centuries*. Macklow Publications
Nobbs, George 1988 *Norwich City Hall*. Norwich City Council
Norwich 12 www.norwich12.co.uk
Norwich HEART (Heritage, Economic & Regeneration Trust), www.heritagecity.org
Penfold, Saul 2006 *Norwich Cathedral*. Jarrold Publishing
Pevsner, Nikolaus 1962 *The buildings of England: North-East Norfolk and Norwich*. Penguin Books
Phillips, Elaine 1999 *A Short History of the Great Hospital*. Jarrold Bookprint
Rawcliffe, Carole and Wilson, Richard (eds) 2004 *Medieval Norwich*. Hambledon and London
Rawcliffe, Carole and Wilson, Richard with Clark, Christine (eds) 2004 *Norwich since 1550*. Hambledon and London
Roman Catholic Cathedral of St John the Baptist, www.stjohncathedral.co.uk
Stephenson, Andrew (ed Jan King) 2004 *A History of the Assembly House*. The Larks Press
Sutermeister, Helen 1977 *The Norwich Blackfriars*. City of Norwich in conjunction with the Norwich Survey